ID080877Z

Simone Ferrari

THE DOGE'S PALACE

in Venice

SKIRA

Skira editore
SkiraMiniARTbooks

Editor
Eileen Romano

Design
Marcello Francone

Editorial Coordination
Carla Casu

Layout
Anna Cattaneo

Editing
Maria Conconi

Iconographical Research
Marta Tosi

Translation
Sergio Knipe
for *Scriptum*, Rome

First published in Italy in 2010
by Skira Editore S.p.A.
Palazzo Casati Stampa
via Torino 61
20123 Milano
Italy
www.skira.net

Printed and bound in Italy.
First edition

ISBN 978-88-572-0558-8

Front cover
A view of the Ducal Palace
in a photo by Luciano Romano

Facing title page
Carpaccio
The Lion of Saint Mark
(detail), 1516
Oil on canvas, 130 x 368 cm
Musei Civici Veneziani, Venice

On page 92
The Bridge of Sighs, which joins
the prisons to the offices of the
Tribunal inside the Ducal Palace.

Plan of the Palace
Marco Zanella, Certosa di Pavia

Contents

The Doge's Palace in Venice

• THE DOGE'S PALACE

In the extraordinary interplay between historical events and myth that characterizes the *Serenissima* Republic, the Doge's Palace (or Ducal Palace) represents, along with the Basilica of St. Mark, the very heart of Venice, the driving force and symbol of its glorious epic. The development of the two buildings should jointly be interpreted in terms of continuity and consistent diversity. The church, intended to serve as the "Doge's chapel" was saved from the divine fiery bolts that struck and devastated the palace at various times. This building is associated with political and institutional assignments of the highest level: like a cardinal, the Procurator of St. Mark wore a red toga and was addressed as "Your Excellency"; like the doge, he was elected for life.

Venetian civilization is reflected in the character and significance of the two buildings: the basilica follows the great Romanesque tradition of Europe, with an added oriental touch reflecting the refined taste of Byzantium, which exercised such great influence over Venetian art. The Doge's Palace, by contrast, foreshadows those symbols of Italian power which reached their high point between the 14th and 15th century: the *signorie*. Indeed, the building appears as a sort of "Palazzo dei Signori", after that successful and influential model common to all the most representative cities of Italy. Naturally, the characteristics of local power in Venice differed from those in other places: even in its hierarchical and "conservative" character, the Republic distinguished itself from other centres where power was passed down within a single family (such as that of the Medici in Florence).

Besides, the Republic also had a distinct way of organizing and balancing the powers of its various executive bodies. The most prestigious figure was naturally that of the doge, who was chosen among

7

the members of the major aristocratic families. Head of the state, the doge was appointed for life (like a pope) and governed the magistracies of the Republic. The doge apparently played the role of the absolute prince, by virtue of an investiture possessing religious sacredness and deriving from Byzantine ritual. Destined to dwell at the centre of the Doge's Palace in a sumptuous golden setting, the doge was nevertheless required to conform to the strict etiquette attached to his lofty moral function as sovereign of the *Serenissima*.

An initial guarantee limiting the doge's power was the "Ducal oath", by which he swore to follow certain rules, such as non-interference in the appointment of the patriarch. These norms, collected in individual codes, constitute a founding public act in the history of the balancing of the separate powers in Venice. The "oath" ensured the government's vigilant control over the doge and prevented any attempt to make the appointment hereditary or to slip into imprudent nepotism. One of the primary magistracies (which were assigned specific locations in the Doge's Palace) was the Great Council, consisting of Venetian aristocrats over 25 years of age; its members elected the doge and passed the laws. The *Scala d'Oro* (Golden Staircase) of the palace leads to the *Sala del Collegio* (Hall of the College), which was presided over by the doge along with six *Savi* or councillors, the three heads of the *Consiglio dei Dieci* (Council of Ten), and the chancellors. The *Collegio* decided on the most urgent matters and welcomed the most prestigious embassies. Alongside this was the area allotted to the *pregadi,* who were senators assigned a legislative role. Other areas were set aside to house the much-feared Council of Ten and the State Inquisitors.

Giovanni Bellini
Portrait of Doge Leonardo Loredan, circa 1501
Oil on board, 61.5 x 45 cm
The National Gallery, London.
One of the most famous portraits of a doge. The rich brocade and ornate buttons are part of the state robes the sitter is wearing.
The hat, worn over a linen cap, is called "corno" (horn).

IOANNES BELLINVS

• PHASES OF CONSTRUCTION AND TRANSFORMATION

The history of the Palace unfolds across very distinct phases marked by radical transformation, loss, destruction, and dramatic fires. The initial core that was developed from the 9th century onwards, has been lost; what has been preserved is the result of undertakings begun in the 14th century. Behind this new outline lay a specific political logic; for it is in the palace that the system of power consolidated at the time – confined to a limited number of aristocratic families – found its physical and symbolic expression. The planning of the building reflects a "conservative" swing: the "Closure of the Great Council" in 1297 was a clearly restrictive measure which limited access to government offices to certain noble families; through the *Quarantia*, a special magistracy, a strict selection of the ruling class was made; and in 1319, complex regulations were introduced for the right to sit on the Great Council.

Another highly significant date is 1340 when the government allocated a considerable sum for the construction of a huge new hall for the over 1200 members of the Great Council. Apart from the practical necessity of housing a plethora of people, it called for grandeur with a clearly symbolic significance, that would add dignity to the rule of the State and be capable of standing comparison with the *Sala della Ragione* at Padua. A document of the time illustrates the expectations of the commissioners: the work must be carried out punctually; the measurements for the building are laid down; other construction work is scheduled, including rooms for offices, an open arcade, and a new stairway to provide adequate access. Finally, care is taken to make it easier and more comfortable for the doge to move from his own apartment to the *Sala*.

In the early 15th century, thanks to Doge Michele Steno, the façade of the spacious council hall was adorned with a wide balcony: this monumental sculptural work, produced by the Dalle Masegne brothers, presents a sophisticated outline of markedly Gothic taste, rhythmically alternating statues of various kind and vertical cusps, multifoil and lancet arches, and tondos. The imposing structure – almost a reliquary – features a female allegorical figure extending above the palace displaying the attributes of Justice, the sword and scales.

In the course of the centuries, building work was carried out incessantly and with extraordinary results. Under the reign of Doge Tomaso Mocenigo (1414–23), for example, huge expenses were allocated for decorative and redevelopment work. Not long after, in 1443, Bartolomeo Bon created the *Porta della Carta,* a gateway in a flowery Gothic style which was originally brightly coloured and gold-plated. In the mid-15th century work began on the erection of the *Arco Foscari*, a genuine honorary arch inspired by a type in use in ancient Rome and which in the same period Leon Battista Alberti was also adopting in other parts of Italy as a way of adding an original touch to his buildings. Improvements made to prestigious inner rooms (such as the doge's quarters) alternated with outside ones, such as the *Scala dei Giganti* (Stairway of the Giants). Built by Antonio Rizzo at the end of the century and completed with Jacopo Sansovino's statues in 1566, this is a symbolic place for the entire building complex and enables access to the most important areas of the building. From this stairway the doge showed himself to the people after he was elected and from here the Ducal oath was sworn.

Following pages
The fourth side of the Ducal Palace is formed by the wall of the ancient palatine chapel of the Basilica of St. Mark. On the lower left is the group of Tetrarchs, spoil from Constantinople at the time of the Fourth Crusade.

Another splendid period was that of the long reigns of Leonardo Loredan and Andrea Gritti in the 16th century, when the *Cortile dei Senatori* (Courtyard of the Senators) and the *Scala d'Oro* (Golden Stairway) were created. This long – seemingly endless – chain of building work met the saddest of ends with the disastrous fires of 1574 and 1577. An unfortunate fate forever destroyed some of the most representative rooms of the palace and seriously threatened the very skeleton of the building in certain sections; a number of extraordinary paintings were lost by some of the greatest masters – Bellini, Giorgione, and Titian.

With great pride, the *Serenissima* managed to recover from this unlucky turn of fate, resuming the work and carrying it on over the following centuries by engaging illustrious representatives of Venetian art, such as Veronese and Tintoretto. These events, nevertheless, signal a watershed between a glorious past, marked by political and artistic preeminence, and a more uncertain – if not gloomy – future. The epic of the Renaissance had drawn to a close.

● THE PALACE ARCHITECTURE

Construction work between the 14th century and the first half of the 15th gave the building its distinctive appearance, which as a whole can still be admired today.

The imposing mass overlooking the water, as seen from the island of San Giorgio, embodies a fundamental type of Venetian architecture, which served as a model for future developments. Naturally, only single stylistic features could be imitated in the construction of private palaces, for the essential structure, with its vast central courtyard, required an extensive surface area.

14

The Palace is structured on three levels: the walls of the upper level are marked by windows and a central balcony, while below are two alternating series of arches. The specific and innovative character of the overall structure is immediately striking and significantly differs from that found, for instance, in the Tuscan tradition.

In the homeland of Giotto and Brunelleschi, between the Middle Ages and the 15th century, a classicist paradigm was predominant, based on an exact and measured definition of details, on geometrical proportion, and on a feeling of harmony attained through a superior, mathematical and binding norm. This view found its chief ally in drawing, which made it possible to precisely trace contours, while at the same time defining and structuring forms. San Miniato al Monte (12th century) or the façade of Santa Maria Novella, designed by Leon Battista Alberti in 1450, represent absolute paradigms of this new course. The same style also spread in the field of painting, as illustrated for instance by the works of Piero della Francesca and later Michelangelo and Raphael (the latter, while born in Urbino, was closely related to the Tuscan style).

The Venetian architecture of the Doge's Palace is very different. Instead of a single and continuous wall, we here find a more dynamic and complex space; drawing has lost its key role and has been replaced by values such as light, shadow, atmosphere, and effects of vibration and transparency. The "perforated" character of the double series of arches creates a wonderful chiaroscuro effect, with a strongly emotional impact. The kind of perception required on the part of the viewer is also different. In Florentine culture, the architectural space was something that ultimately had to be intellectually understood in its structure and rational exactness. In Venice, by contrast, the use of

15

more subtle colour modulations affects the senses in a more immediate way and requires no cultural cognitive filter. The autonomy and foundation of this tradition occur across the centuries in various forms, from the Doge's Palace to the masterpieces of Giovanni Bellini, Palladio Titian and Veronese. Venetian tonality offers the world a style deliberately alternative to the classical paradigm developed by Tuscan artists. It is no chance, therefore, that the poet D'Annunzio, while lavishing praise on the central-Italian masters, wrote some of his most beautiful and moving pages inspired by what he had seen in Venice: the charming atmospheres of *Il Fuoco* (*The Fire*) could only have been set amidst the sparkling colours of Venetian paintings and the bright reflections of the palaces of the *Serenissima*.

Lazzaro Bastiani
The Arrival of Duke Ercole I d'Este and Alfonso I in Venice from Ferrara, 1487 Museo Correr, Venice. With the Peace of Bagnolo, in 1484, Ercole was forced to cede Polesine and Rovigo to Venice, lands that had been fought over during the war begun in 1482.

What also cannot pass unobserved in the building is its explicit and exhibited adoption of a double register of Gothic arches: a choice that when compared to normative Tuscan models – which preferred the semi-circular, round arch to its "wicked", "medieval", "Greek", "Gothic" or "barbarian" alternative – might appear as a challenge. Actually, this choice represents a conscious cultural rejection that illustrates how Venetian architecture belonged to a different tradition from that of the early Florentine Renaissance, one that may be described as late Gothic or international Gothic. Certainly this was not a marginal style but rather an alternative, common in many European areas, which sought to recover medieval values and the preciosity of Gothic with its decorative, flowery taste not subordinated to the structural logic of space. Within this current we find some splendid works, such as those of Masolino da Panicale, Gentile da Fabriano, or the interior of Santa Maria delle Grazie in Milan.

The two main façades of the Ducal Palace overlook the Piazzetta and the waterfront. The fretwork character of the double series of arches creates a wonderful chiaroscuro effect. Despite the variety tripartition brings, the building presents an harmonious structure which derives from some formal correspondences introduced in the two series of arches. Each arch in the lower part is matched by two above, in such a way as to create a sequence of 1:2.

On the basis of a Renaissance logic of pure artistic progress that calls for conformity to the "winning" innovations of Tuscan genius, it is impossible to understand the charming insertion above the arches on the central façade of the Doge's Palace of a quatrefoil enclosed within a circle: a purely aesthetic choice that serves no functional or static purpose. Despite the diversity brought by its tripartition, the façade presents an intrinsic harmony, which derives from certain formal correspondences introduced by the two sequences of arches. Each arch present on the lower level is matched by two arches on the upper one, in such a way as to form a 1:2 sequence.

It is as if this part of the building were formed by a series of rectangles whose base is the distance between the columns of the lower level and whose height coincides with the overall height of the two arches, which is to say the distance between the base of the building and the decoration above the quatrefoiled tondos. These rectangles repeat a module, a geometrical pattern that gives harmony to the whole building: not a static or monotonous harmony, but one that is rhythmical, dynamic and embellished by a skillful use of chiaroscuro.

Building work on the Doge's Palace – which continued over several centuries until the final touches were added in the 18th century – became a dramatic and compelling necessity in the late 16th century because of the aforementioned fires of the 1570s, which caused serious damage not only to the pictorial decorations but also to the very structure of the palace. Long deliberations were held on whether the building was to be retained or demolished and rebuilt, in whole or in part: the issue was political as well as strictly technical, and the Senate sought the opinion of many architects. In the end the decision was made to renovate the old Gothic structure, in homage to tradition and in some measure for good luck: Francesco Sansovino, the son of the architect and sculptor Jacopo, argued that the palazzo had been "founded under favourable stars by their fathers and ancients: since the Republic from that time to the present has always grown in power and greatness (…) I would think it grave to leave it, as it has given fortune and happiness".

An investigation made by the Venetian architect Giovanni Antonio Rusconi was decisive; in his opinion the damage caused by the fire was no more than a small mosquito bite on an elephant.

The façades were therefore preserved. The tracery of the windows damaged by fire was removed, but this procedure spoiled the balance between the lower and upper part of the façade, the upper part appearing top heavy. This can be seen even today, in particular looking at the southern façade, where the original tracery of two windows is preserved.

● PICTORIAL RENEWAL

From Bellini to Titian, from Tintoretto to Tiepolo, all the masters of Venetian painting were contacted at various stages to renew and embellish the rooms of the Doge's Palace. Among the many works painted by the greatest representative of the Venetian Quattrocento, Giovanni Bellini, only one was spared from the raging fire of 1577, the wonderful *Lamentation over the Dead Christ*. Already mentioned by Ridolfi (1648) as present in the rooms of the *Avogadria di Comun*, a magistracy whose role it was to keep watch over equality among aristocrats, the painting was later moved at various times to other areas of the Doge's Palace and is presently displayed in the *Sala dei Ritratti* (Portrait Hall), of the doge's apartment. Dated to around 1472, this

21

is a tempera painting on canvas and is now in a poor state of conservation. Nevertheless, it represents a milestone in the career of the Venetian painter. What is striking is the marked illusionism of its altar-sarcophagus, as seen from below – a feature that recalls the daring perspective experiments of Andrea Mantegna (since 1453 Bellini's brother-in-law), the author of bold innovations from the 1450s onwards, as illustrated by his frescoes for the *Camera degli Sposi* at Mantua and his famous *Lamentation over the Dead Christ*, now at Brera. The tag folded under the body of Christ, and bearing Bellini's signature, contributes to the spatial and prospective dimension of the painting. Also extraordinary is the highly dramatic expressive rendition of the scene: a unique pathos, of the kind rarely found in Italy, and which is a good match for the works of the great Flemish masters such as Rogier van der Weyden. These artists were well known and highly appreciated in Italy, particularly by Venetian collectors. Michele Vianello owned Jan van Eyck's *The Crossing of the Red Sea*, while in 1451 an altarpiece by Petrus Christus could be seen in the Church of the Carità. Giovanni Bellini must have known these paintings and a great many others, and studied them with great interest.

Canaletto

Stairway of the Giants in the Ducal Palace (detail), 1765
Private collection, Mexico City.
A symbol for the entire structure, this stairway leads to the most prestigious rooms of the building and is where the doge showed himself to the people after he was elected.

Such an important building could hardly lack a contribution from one of the greatest of 16th century artists: Tiziano Vecellio (Titian), who painted a fresco of *Saint Christopher* for Doge Andrea Gritti (1523–38). This painting is dominated by a plastic definition of the human figure, which is given volumetric prominence and a muscular, anatomic tension worthy of the greatest mannerists. In the works produced in this period, Titian draws inspiration from the great paragons

Façade overlooking the waterfront. This is the oldest part of the Ducal Palace; the central balcony by Pier Paolo Dalle Masegne, dating from the years 1400–04, was suitably integrated with the 14th-century architectural framework.

of Roman painting: Michelangelo and Raphael. A mannerist engagement with these prototypes had not long before been shown by Pordenone, who in various instances may have served as a model for Titian himself. Besides this central-Italian component, the fresco is marked by the completely personal style of the master. In the background is an actual depiction of St. Mark's Basin, with the Bell Tower and Doge's Palace. This represents a most precocious and quite modern experiment, which paved the way for the future development of a new artistic genre – landscape painting – which was made famous in the 18th century by Canaletto, Guardi and Bellotto.

Another undisputed star of this period is Tintoretto, an industrious and most successful painter who worked on various rooms of the Palace. In the four canvases he painted for the *Anticollegio* (Antechamber), for instance, Tintoretto displayed many of his artistic virtues: the mythological scenes present here were developed through skillful, almost theatrical prospective control. In *Mercury and the Three Graces* the figures stretch out and bend as if to conform to a pre-imposed compositional rhythm, of clear mannerist origin. The praise of coiled forms, so fashionable in Florence, here finds one of its best accomplished examples. The muscular and anatomical tension of the figures betrays a clear admiration on the artist's part for Michelangelo's cult of form. Tintoretto's mannerism, both rhetorical and theatrical, feeds on an ongoing luminous tension: it is the use of light – flickering, spectacular and strongly directed – that distinguishes Tintoretto from his colleagues. This light serves to construct, reveal and identify depending on the occasion, and is employed wisely and with extraordinary craftiness; it lends the representation further emphasis and contributes to the magniloquence of the visual language and subjects portrayed. The wealth of components and the variety of layouts, combined with his feel for volumes, colour and light, made Tintoretto an outstanding exemplar for the great art of the 17th century proposed by Annibale Carracci.

The swan-song of the centuries-old epic of the *Serenissima* and of the Doge's Palace came at the close of the 18th century with the work of the greatest painter of the century: Giambattista Tiepolo. His painting *Neptune Offering Gifts to Venice* represents a synthesis of his qualities. At ease with any kind of subject, whether religious or mythological, the artist displayed a joyous and most happy feel for colour and a brushstroke marked by a rich impasto that made him the only worthy heir to the tradition of Veronese. Caught between *chiaristi* and *tenebrosi*, Tiepolo sided with the former: the quality of his work, with its diaphanous hues and lightness of touch made Tiepolo a popular and acclaimed painter throughout Europe. The Doge's Palace could hardly fail to offer an example of his work.

One last artist of importance, and one who gives the history of the palace a European dimension, is the disturbing and phantasmagorical Bosch. Four of his paintings are preserved in the building. The presence of the Flemish artist in Venice in the late 15th century had a profound impact on the artistic development of the city. His marvellous lighting effects, nocturnal scenes, dazzling moonlights and flickering reflections influenced Giorgione, Titian and Lotto, among many others.

● THE TRIUMPH OF VERONESE

In 16th-century Venice, the indisputable primacy of Titian was only limited by the shining figure of Paolo Veronese. Before the versatile touch of this artist the most industrious and influential members of

27

the nobility bowed gratefully: Giustinian, Contarini, Barbaro, Pisani, Soranzo – only to mention a few prominent families. Paintings and frescoes by Veronese can be admired in the most prestigious buildings, from the Libreria Marciana to Villa Barbaro at Maser; from the Church of San Sebastiano to great museum across the world. The reasons for Veronese's success are many and easy to grasp. The modern viewer, like that of the 16th century, will gaze with amazement at a universe fashioned by an inexhaustible imaginativeness, which creates an endless number of shapes, colours, perspective cuts, compositional horizons, gestures, decorations, and adornments.

Jacopo Sansovino
Golden Staircase,
1555–59
A continuation of the *Giant's Staircase*, it is named for its vaulted ceiling, which is richly decorated in white stucco and gold leaf.
It was reserved for use by Magistrates and high-ranking people.

Embracing license as something more important in painting than the demands of propriety, Veronese epitomizes a number of qualities: virtuosity, gestural rhetoric, theatricality, the transcending of the limits of human anatomy, luminism, and bold and daring perspectives. Born in 1528, he had received official acknowledgment while still a young man – not yet thirty. His first assignment for the Doge's Palace dates to 1553–55 and was followed by others in the years 1576–78 and 1579–82.

This continuing connection with the building most representative of the Republic – of its government and system of power – made Veronese the greatest painter of the *Serenissima* at a time when this sought to create a mythical and idealized image of itself through encomiastic and decorative projects of the highest level. In the central canvases (the lateral ones are works by Giambattista Zelotti and Giovanni Battista Ponchino) of the ceiling of the *Sala delle Udienze* (Audience Hall) of the most respected and feared local magistracy, the *Consiglio dei Dieci*, Veronese displayed all his power by engaging with

29

mythology, one of the privileged subjects of narrative painting. References to the gods of Olympus aim to revive the myth of Venice, and to send clear message – a genuine warning – to other Italian and European powers. The pagan gods, foreshortened through a virtuoso perspective from the bottom up, clearly show benevolence towards the *Serenissima*: Juno pours gifts of all sorts – crowns, jewels, and gold coins – on resplendent Venice. In the central canvas (a copy by Jacopo d'Andrea; the original is now in the Louvre) Jove himself chases the Vices beyond the horizon, while underneath, in a painting by Zelotti, *Liberty Breaks the Shackles* under the aegis of Mercury, a veritable tutelary deity, which had already been consecrated as a symbol of the city in Jacopo de' Barbari's *Bird's-eye View* (1500), now in the Correr Museum.

Following these initial assignments, the painter was engaged for the decoration of the adjacent hall, the *Sala della Bussola* (Compass Chamber), the antechamber used by the *Consiglio dei Dieci* and the inquisitors. Here the artist painted *Saint Mark Crowning the Theological Virtues* (Faith, Hope and Charity), on display at the Louvre since 1797 (it has been replaced by a copy). Moving on to the third hall, that of the *Tre Capi del Consiglio dei Dieci* (Three Heads of the Council of Ten), we find works by the master marked by dynamic and repeated effects, as well as daring formulations centred on diagonals, excited and tumultuous movements, strained and unexpected perspective, virtuoso views, and iridescent and dazzling colours. In contrast to the classical approach of Venetian painting – the stress on tonality first introduced by Giovanni Bellini in the 15th century that led to the warm hues of Titian – Veronese adopts an approach of his own, where a revival of the classicist paradigm is combined with a mannerist style.

The best known and most representative works by Veronese, however, are those in the *Sala del Collegio* and the *Sala del Maggior Consiglio*. In the former hall – which Palladio restored after the fire of 1574 – Veronese painted his *Sebastiano Venier giving thanks to the Redeemer after the Battle of Lepanto*, a consecration of the eagerly awaited victory of the Republic against its Turkish enemy. An encomiastic painting, it represents the high point in the "political" engagement of the artist, who here shed praise on the protagonists of the victorious naval battle, Sebastiano Venier and Agostino Barbarigo, shown as – together with Venice – they worship Christ, Emperor of the World. Veronese worked on the *Sala del Maggior Consiglio* after the disastrous fire of 1577, when he painted a grand oval (9 × 6 meters!) with the *Apotheosis of Venice*: the triumph of a city, accompanied by angels and Virtues, but also that of a painter who had reached the peak of his fame and had proved capable of achieving astonishing and masterly effects through his perspective views from the bottom up, choice of settings and dazzling colours.

Following pages
Giovanni Bellini
Pietà (detail), *circa* 1472
Sala dei Ritratti.
Among the many works
executed by the artist, this
one – still to be found in
the Ducal Palace – is the
only one to have survived
the terrible fire of 1577.

Guided Tour

1. Scala dei Giganti

Once the entrance of honour, this *Stairway of the Giants* was first designed by Antonio Rizzo between 1483 and 1485 and then completed with sculptured feature in 1491. It takes its name from the two statues of Mars and Neptune sculpted by Jacopo Sansovino in 1565, and which symbolize the power of Venice over land and sea. This stairway is where the ceremony for the coronation of the doge took place.

2. Sala del Maggior Consiglio

The Hall of the Great Council is the largest in the Palace, where the most important magistracy of Venice used to meet. In 1577, it was badly damaged by a fire that had broken out in the nearby Sala dello Scrutinio. A decorative project was undertaken with the work of artists such as Veronese, Tintoretto and Palma Giovane.

VERONESE
The Triumph of Venice (whole work and detail on following pages), 1582 Oil on canvas, 904 x 580 cm The painting is a depiction of the apotheosis of the city, crowned by angels and surrounded by Virtues. Below, the various members of Venetian society are shown.

TINTORETTO
Paradise, 1588–92
Oil on canvas,
700 x 2000 cm

Despite its vast size, the Hall has no inner supporting columns: its ceiling is sustained by a clever system of trusses and beams. The spaciousness of the room reflects its function as the place where the supreme assembly of the state met, which included up to 2,000 members. The platform with the Doge's seat was located against the background wall.

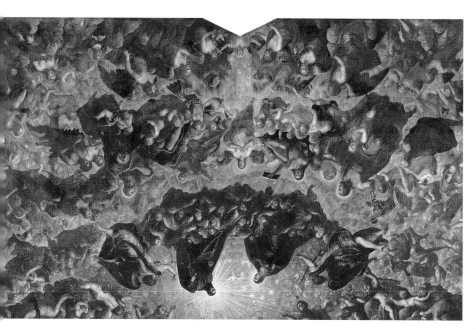

TINTORETTO
Paradise (details),
1588–92

Behind the throne extends
the largest canvas in the
world. This was painted by
Tintoretto and his workshop
to replace a fresco by
Guariento that had been
destroyed in the fire of
1577. The artist completed
the painting piece by piece
in his San Marziale

workshop, with much help
from his assistants, and
particularly his son
Domenico, who took care
of the final assemblage of
the canvases. At the centre,
the Virgin intercedes with
Christ on the behalf of
Venice; surmounted by
the dove of the Holy Spirit,
she is supported by a dense
formation of cherubs and
seraphs in a semicircle.

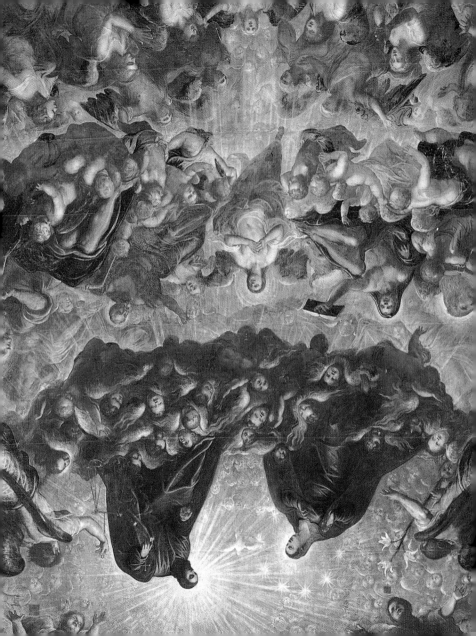

JACOPO PALMA
THE YOUNGER
*The Crusader army
attacks Constantinople,*
circa 1587
Oil on canvas

The episodes of Venetian
history frescoed in the
Sala del Maggior Consiglio
refer to relations with the
Papacy and the Empire;
the ceiling shows the
deeds of valorous citizens
and the Virtues, while the
central space is reserved
for the glorification of the
Republic. The twelve side
paintings, six on each wall,
depict particular deeds or
episodes of war during the
city's history; the work
here is an example.

Portraits of Doges Antonio Grimani and Andrea Gritti Below the ceiling of the *Sala del Maggior Consiglio* runs a frieze with the portraits of the first 77 doges of Venice (the others can be found in the *Sala dello Scrutinio*). These are imaginary portraits, as those executed before 1577 by Jacopo and Domenico Tintoretto were destroyed in the fire. On the scroll that each doge holds in his hands are listed the most important achievements of his reign.

3. Sala dello Scrutinio

This spacious hall was originally intended to house the manuscripts Petrarch and Bessarion had bequeathed to the Republic; hence, it was once known as *Sala della Libreria* (Library Hall). Then in 1532 it was chosen as the place where the *scrutini* (ballots) were to be held, which is to say the political elections, including that of the doge. The walls of the hall illustrate the battles Venice won between 809 and 1656. In the frieze below the ceiling there continues the list of doges that starts in the *Sala del Maggior Consiglio*, while the southern wall of the hall is adorned with Palma il Giovane's *Last Judgment* (1594–95).

4. Sala dello Scudo

This hall takes its name from the fact that it was the place where the coat of arms (*scudo*) of the ruling doge was displayed, and it was here that he gave audiences and receive his guests. On its two main walls are four maps and a few paintings illustrating the voyages of the most famous Venetian explorers.

FRANCESCO GRISELLINI AND GIUSTINO MENESCARDI, *Mare Mediterraneum, Arabia, Egypt, Palestine, Syria, Cilicia, and Cyprus*, 1762
Oil on canvas

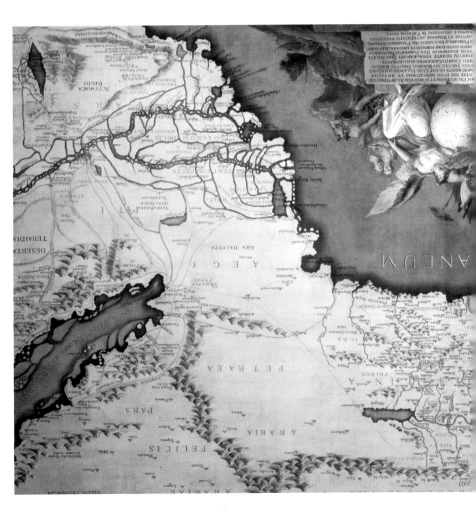

FRANCESCO GRISELLINI
AND GIUSTINO
MENESCARDI
*Greenland, Iceland,
Sweden, Italy, Greece
and Asia Minor* (detail),
1762. Oil on canvas
Besides the large maps, at the centre of the
room are two globes
with the celestial vault
and the terrestrial,
illustrating how the power
of Venice rested on
an illustrious and glorious
tradition.

53

5. Sala Grimani

VITTORE CARPACCIO
The Lion of Saint Mark,
1516
Oil on canvas, 130 x 368 cm

This hall takes its name
from the coat of arms
(featured in the centre of
the ceiling) of the Grimani,
a powerful family that gave
the Republic three doges.
On the walls important
paintings have been
collected depicting
the *Lion of Saint Mark,*
including the famous
one by Carpaccio. In the
background of this painting
are the lagoon and the
edifices of the Piazza
overlooking the Basin:
the Campanile, Clock
Tower, Basilica and Ducal
Palace. On the right are
galeazze; large rowing or
sailing galleys that ensured
Venetian rule of the seas.

HIERONYMUS BOSCH *Triptych of the hermits*, *Saint Jerome* (central panel) and, on the opposite page *Saint Anthony* (left panel), *Saint Giles* (right panel), *1505*

Oil on board, triptych, 86.5 x 30 cm In the early sixteenth century great European artists such as Leonardo da Vinci, Michelangelo, Albrecht Dürer and

Hieronymus Bosch visited Venice. After his sojourn in Venice Bosch favoured broader compositions, which were nonetheless rich in bizarre and fantastical imagery.

This triptych is perhaps the artist's most important painting from his stay in Venice. The work portrays the three saints Anthony, Jerome and Giles as models of integrity.

The first saint is depicted as he refuses to give in to temptations tormenting his ascetic meditations, while the second prays among the ruins of a pagan temple. The third saint is painted with an arrow through his breast, which was fated for an innocent doe shown at his feet. The landscape widens atmospherically to a deep, natural view.

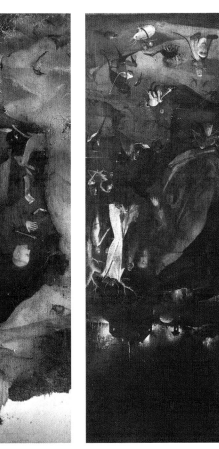

Previous pages
HIERONYMUS BOSCH
Triptych of the hermits
(open), *Saint Jerome*
(detail), 1505
Oil on board, triptych,
86.5 x 60 cm

HIERONYMUS BOSCH
Triptych of the Crucified
Martyr, (open), *Crucified*
Martyr (detail), 1500–04
Oil on board, 104 x 119 cm.

HIERONYMUS BOSCH
Triptych of the Crucified
Martyr, (open), *Saint*
Anthony, The Crucified
Martyr, Monk and Soldier
(whole work and detail),
circa 1497 or later
Oil on board, 104 x 119 cm
Aside from the serious
damage it has suffered
from fire, this painting shows
incongruities between
its side panels and the
central one. This has made
it difficult to interpret
the narrated episode
and identify the female
saint portrayed.

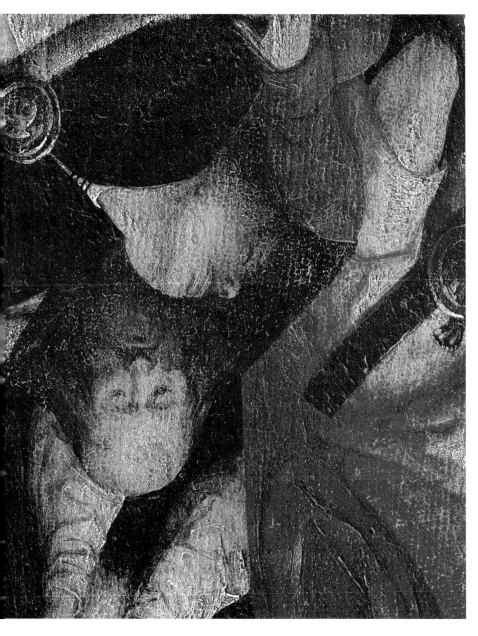

HIERONYMUS BOSCH
Triptych of the Crucified Martyr

On the central panel is a depiction of the martyrdom of the female saint before a crowd. On the left, at the feet of the cross, is a man who has fainted: if the scene is interpreted as illustrating the martyrdom of St. Julia, then this should be the merchant Eusebius; if it is interpreted as the martyrdom of St. Liberata, the unconscious man might be the saint's father, the King of Portugal, who sentenced her to martyrdom.

7. Sala delle Quattro Porte

This hall takes its name from its four doors, framed by precious oriental marbles and surmounted by group statues. The ceiling — with a barrel vault decorated with stucco

work by Giovanni Cambi (known as "Il Bombarda") — is marked by frescoes with mythological scenes and the cities and regions under Venetian rule, which were executed by Jacopo Tintoretto from 1578,

TITIAN
The Doge Grimani adoring Faith, 157–75
Oil on canvas, 373 x 496 cm
This room owes its present appearance to the reconstruction that followed the terrible fire of 1574 and which was carried out under the direction of Antonio da Ponte and according to Palladio's plan, with paintings by Tintoretto, Titian and Tiepolo. The hall served as a passageway and waiting room for those granted an audience by the Senate and Signoria.

GIAMBATTISTA TIEPOLO
*Neptune Offering Gifts
to Venice*, 1758
Oil on canvas, 135 x 275 cm
Sala delle Quattro Porte.
Venice is dressed like
a late 16th century
noblewoman: adorned
with jewels, she wears
a ceremonial dress with
the ermine cape of the
doge and holds the sceptre
of military power in
her hand. The pearls
on her neck – like the coral
and gold pouring out from
Neptune's horn of plenty –
give confirmation of the fact
that the sea has always
been the source of the
Serenissima's wealth.

8. Sala dell'Anticollegio

This was the antechamber of honour for ambassadors and delegations waiting to be received by the Collegio.

TINTORETTO
Minerva Sending Away

Mars from Peace and Prosperity, 1577–78
Oil on canvas, 148 x 168 cm
On the side of the doors are four canvases which Tintoretto painted for the Atrio Quadrato, and which were moved

here in 1716 to replace the original decoration of the hall.
The scenes have an allegorical meaning and refer to the good government of the *Serenissima* Republic.

TINTORETTO

Mercury and the Three Graces, 1577–78
Oil on canvas, 146 x 167 cm
These canvases, intended
to extol the notion of union
and concord, and also
possess a cosmological

meaning which links them
to the Seasons depicted
on the ceiling: the presence
of *Mercury and the Three
Graces* should be seen
as evoking spring and the
element of air.

TINTORETTO

*Bacchus and Ariadne
Crowned by Venus,*
1577-78
Oil on canvas, 146 x 167 cm

This painting should be
seen as illustrating both the symbolic marriage between Venice and the Adriatic Sea, which was renewed each year during the feast of the Assumption, and the season of autumn.

VERONESE
The Rape of Europa,
circa 1580
Oil on canvas, 240 x 303 cm
After falling in love with the
Phoenician princess Europa,
Jove decided to seize her in
the guise of a bull. In the
foreground, the beautiful
princess, having overcome
her initial fear, sits confident
and unaware upon the false
bull who is licking her foot in
a loving kiss.

JACOPO BASSANO
Jacob's Return to Canaan,
1580
Oil on canvas, 150 x 205 cm
known as Jacopo Bassano,
Jacopo da Ponte,
established a new genre
by introducing rural
themes in sacred
representations, to the
point of turning these
into pastoral scenes.

9. Sala del Collegio

This hall was intended to house the meetings of the *Collegio dei Savi* and of the *Serenissima Signoria*, bodies charged with administrative duties and the representation of the State. The decorative work was completed after the fire of 1574 according to Andrea Palladio's plan.

VERONESE
Sebastiano Venier giving thanks to the Redeemer after the Battle of Lepanto, 1581–82
Oil on canvas, 285 x 565 cm
On the back wall is a vast and sophisticated allegory with saints Sebastian and Justine in chiaroscuro on the sides. The leaders of the naval victory of Lepanto, Sebastiano Venier (later elected doge) and Agostino Barbarigo, are shown worshipping Christ, Emperor of the World, along with Venice, St. Mark, St. Justine and Faith, amid rejoicing martyrs and saints.

JOSEPH HEINTZ
THE YOUNGER
(circa 1600–78)
*Dogal Audience in the
Sala del Collegio*
Oil on canvas, 57 x 64 cm
Venice, Museo Correr.
The chief duty of the
Collegio was that of
directing and coordinating
the Senate by reading
the dispatches from
ambassadors and rectors,
receiving foreign
delegations and promoting
legislative and political
work.

VERONESE
Venice Enthroned with Justice and Peace, 1577–78
Oil on canvas, 250 x 180 cm

VERONESE
Mars and Neptune, 1577–78
Oil on canvas, 250 x 180 cm
This ceiling is one of the artist's masterpieces;

it extolls the Good Government of the Republic, the Faith on which it rested and the Virtues that guided it.

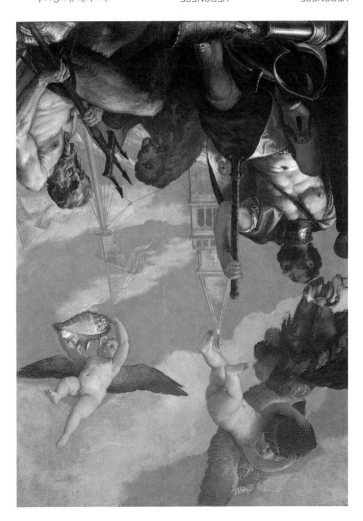

VERONESE
Dialectic (whole work
and detail), 1577–78
Oil on canvas,
150 x 200 cm
All around the hall,
on eight T and L-shaped
panels the Virtues of
Government are shown.

80

10. Sala del Senato

Also known as the *Sala dei Pregadi* – for the doge would "pray" members to attend meetings – this hall housed the gatherings of the Senate, one of the oldest institutions of Venice.

TINTORETTO
Venice Enthroned as Queen of the Sea, 1587–94
Oil on canvas, 810 x 420 cm
The deities surrounding Venice represent the members of the assembly of the *Consiglio*.

Following pages
Wall clock divided into 24 hours.
Wall clock showing the position of the Sun in the Zodiac.

11. Sala del Consiglio dei Dieci

The Council of Ten was established after the plot certain nobles laid in 1310 to overthrow state institutions, but soon became a permanent body with authority over all sectors of public life. Its assembly was formed by ten members chosen from the Senate and elected by the *Maggior Consiglio*, as well as the doge and his six advisors – hence the seventeen panels arranged in a semicircle that are still visible in the hall.

VERONESE
*Juno Bestowing Her Gifts
on Venice* (whole work
and detail), 1553–56
Oil on canvas,
365 × 147 cm

In this painting, Venice
is depicted as a young
lady dressed "in modern
fashion" on whom Juno
pours insignias – the
Ducal horn, a crown,
money and jewels – that
signify her power. At
Venice's feet is the Lion,
the symbol of the city.

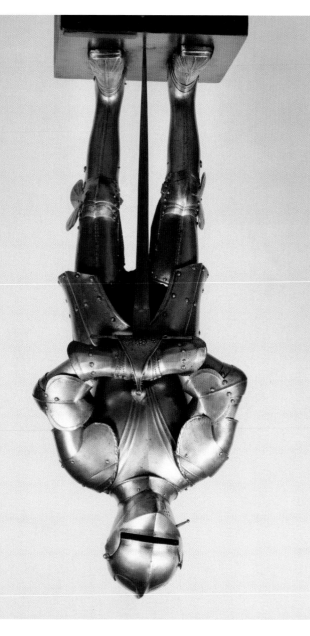

12. Armoury

Boy's armour, Renaissance period.

In Hall I, known as "Sala del Gattamelata", 16th-century armour is on display for light and heavy combat on horseback or foot, as well as for tournaments. A curious item is a boy's (or midget's) armour that was found on the battlefield of Marignano in 1515.

These series of halls, which were originally conceived as a storehouse for the armigers of the Palace, are today a precious museum of weapons and munitions of various provenance, with over 2,000 items. In Hall III it is worth noting the culverin, a small and finely decorated cannon from the mid-16th century.

Appendix

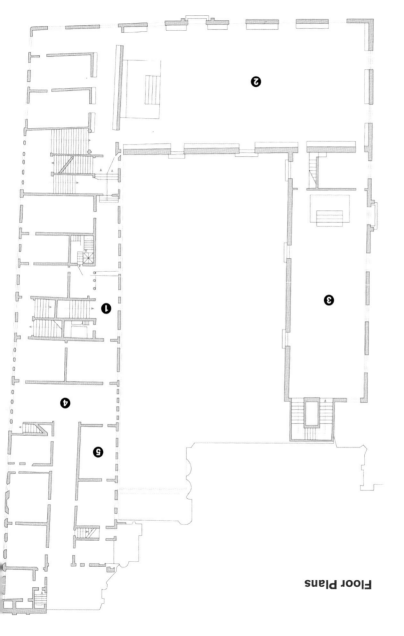

Floor Plans

First Floor

1. Scala dei Giganti
(*Stairway of the Giants*)
2. Sala del Maggior Consiglio
(*Hall of the Great Council*)
3. Sala dello Scrutinio
(*Hall of the Ballots*)
4. Sala dello Scudo
(*Hall of the Coat of Arms*)
5. Sala Grimani
(*Grimani Hall*)

Second Floor

6. Sala del Magistrato
dei Conservatori alle leggi
7. Sala delle Quattro Porte
(*Hall of the Four Doors*)
8. Sala dell'Anticollegio
(*Hall of the Antechamber*)
9. Sala del Collegio
(*Hall of the College*)
10. Sala del Senato
(*Hall of the Senate*)
11. Sala del Consiglio dei Dieci
(*Hall of the Council of Ten*)
12. Armeria
(*Armoury*)

0   10 m

95

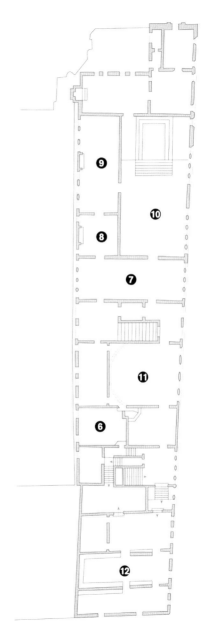

Further Information

Palazzo Ducale
San Marco 1
30124 Venezia
Tel. (+39) 041 2715911

Visitors' Entrance
Porta del Frumento, Piazzetta San Marco

Opening Hours
From Novemer 1 to March 31
9 am – 6 pm (ticket office 9 am – 5 pm);
From April 1 to October 31
9 am – 7 pm (ticket office 9 am – 6 pm)
Closed December 25, January 1

Wheelchair and stroller accessible
(except for the Prison and the Armoury).

Guided and audio tours available.

www.museicivicivicveneziani.it